I give thanks to all the loss I have experienced in life, for the gifts contained in those moments and the growth and strength I have found within myself as a result. Thank you x

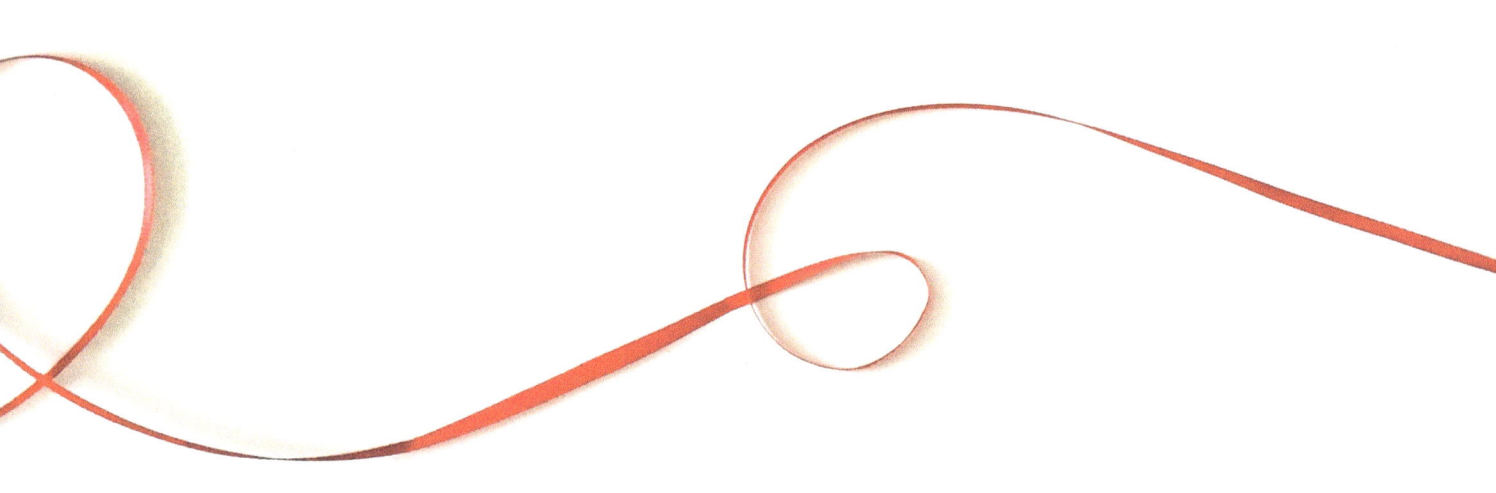

Copyright © Shirley Harvey 2016
All rights reserved. No part of this book may be reproduced, transmitted, or stored in an information retrieval system in any form or by any means, graphic, electronic, or mechanical, including photocopying, taping, and recording, without prior written permission from the publisher.

First edition 2016
ISBN 978-0-9950477-3-0

Published by Shirley World Publications in a magical place called Shirley World.
www.shirleyharvey.com

Written and Illustrated by Shirley Harvey

One day when I was just walking along,

Minding my business and singing a song,

I found myself falling from the greatest height

With no way to stop it, try as I might.

My song was ripped right out of my mouth

And my feet gave way as I headed south.

I had no way of knowing how it would end

Or, if I survived, would I be able to mend?

Bam! Just like that, it came to a stop

And it hit me so suddenly with a tremendous whop!

The impact whacked everything in me outside

And I lay there in pieces, unable to hide.

The pain so intense it was too much to feel

And I could not make sense of this horrid ordeal.

It struck me I'd just lost my bestest friend

And this whole ordeal was not at an end.

At the time I could see there was no sense at all

In accepting my circumstance, accepting my fall,

So I pretended it just hadn't happened to me,

That all was well, as well as could be.

I put on a brave face and got back to my walk,

My song had gone but I was able to talk,

Convincing myself, and others too,

That I just had the sniffles because I had flu.

But then I was mad and I started to shout,

"It's not fair! It's wrong!" with my biggest pout.

I stomped around looking for someone to blame,

Someone to scream at, to name and shame,

And sometimes, for a minute or two, it would stick,

An insult I'd hurl, a target I'd hit.

But I realised inside the relief didn't last,

That the impact came back like a blast from the past.

The flu came and went, but the sniffles remained,

Try as I might, they could not be contained.

When I thought I was empty and could cry no more

A new well was found and my tears would pour.

Sometimes my sadness would be raw and strong

And sometimes a melancholy, gentle and long.

In the sorrow and tears I found a tiny release,

A moment of comfort, a moment of peace.

Yet slowly but surely things started to change
And I found a feeling that was novel and strange.
It was peaceful and yielding, patient and kind,
The sort of feeling one doesn't mind.
It came in moments of anger and fear.
It came in sadness and moments of cheer.
A gentle acceptance of all that came,
Of all my emotions and no more blame.

Then, crashing right out of the blue with surprise,

A wave of emotions would come, tell me lies.

They'd tell me I couldn't go on any more

So I'd fall again, find myself on the floor.

But I'd find a way to get back on my feet

And sometimes I'd hear the faintest beat –

The thud of my heart or a distant song,

I couldn't quite tell because it sounded all wrong.

It wasn't a sound I had heard before

But the more I heard it, I wanted it more.

This new beat intrigued me, made me take note,

Like a distant land viewed from a boat.

A landscape that seemed familiar to me,

But things were different from what I could see.

It edged me forward, slowly at first,

Reminding me that I'd once had a great thirst

For life and adventure, exploration and fun,

And that maybe this wasn't the end I'd begun.

Maybe this loss was about something bigger -

An idea, a thought I needed to figure?

So I took a big breath, my mouth opened wide,

And I beckoned my song from deep down inside.

It came with memories, sad and sweet,

And it came with the most distinctive beat,

A beat I remember of my bestest friend

And I realised his song would never end.

Because he passed it to me and to all he knew,

A melody so strong it stuck like glue,

And it merged with my song like a beautiful duet,

Singing something new not discovered yet.

I knew, in that moment, that I would mend,

Not the same as before but better, my friend,

Because now I could sing a more beautiful song

With the beat of my heart, powerful and strong.

Now I could sing a richer song

That would give me strength my whole life long.

trust in all of life
x

Shirley is an artist, writer, entrepreneur and mother with a sweet and whimsical take on the world.

Using her unique style of painting and writing, and her team of trusted animal friends, she brings to light the finer qualities and quirks of what it means to be human with humour and grace.

www.shirleyharvey.com

www.ingramcontent.com/pod-product-compliance
Lightning Source LLC
LaVergne TN
LVHW071033070426
835507LV00003B/134